QUESTIONS OF FIRE

QUESTIONS OF FIRE

Gregg Mosson

Plain View Press
P. O. 42255
Austin, TX 78704

plainviewpress.net
sb@plainviewpress.net
512-441-2452

Copyright © Gregg Mosson 2009. All rights reserved.
ISBN: 978-0-9819731-7-3
Library of Congress Number: 2009925823

No part of this book may be reproduced in any form without permission from the publisher or author, except to quote a passage in a review or for educational classroom use.

Cover painting: *Diminishing Returns*, by Minás Konsolas
  Mixed media on canvas, 2006
Interior design by Pam Knight and Gregg Mosson

First printing, 2009

CONTENTS

Acknowledgements   7

I: LANDSCAPE

Words   13
War Mongers   14
A World Without Picasso's *Guernica*   15
While You're Shopping, Bombs Are Dropping   16
Sight   17
Poem for the Living   18
Memory, June 1942   22
Childhood From a Car   23
Practice   24
Balmy   25
Sunspots   26
October Rain   27
Urban Renewal   28
Long Distance Runner   29
August Hike in Baltimore   32

II: COMMUTING THROUGH DARKNESS

Vantage on a Saturday   39
To a Co-Worker (While Drinking a Beer)   40
I Saw the Moon   41
S.U.V. With Landscape   42
Maneuver for Position   43
Title Yourself   44
Depression at 7 A.M.   45
Song for the Earth   46
Meditation on Washington D.C. in April 2003   50
Caution for Monuments   51
Automation of Sleepwalkers   52
Age Without Heroes   53
That Movie Was So to Die For   54
New Hucksters   55
Mister X Muses in the Mirror   56

III: LIGHT

Music of Questions	61
Reading Adrienne Rich's *Dark Fields of the Republic*	62
Self Portrait at Thirty One	63
Riding to the Anti-War March, New York City, March 20, 2004	67
Portrait of Home	70
Unknown Soldier	71
Sketch From a Hilltop	72
Against *Guantanamo*	73
Fragment	74
Questions Rising Like Smoke	75
End Notes	81
About the Author	83
About the Artist	85

ACKNOWLEDGEMENTS

I want to thank the international Independent Media movement; the U.S. Poets Against War movement and instigating poet Sam Hamill; the D.C. Guerrilla Poetry Insurgency; Marcus Colasurdo and all the keen spirits of his home-cooked workshop; Rosemary Klein for her editing; and publisher Susan Bright and the Plain View Press team for their support.

On February 15, 2003, tens of millions of people around the world marched to reject the U.S. invasion of Iraq—which began on March 19 that same year; this book takes root in those two days.

These poems first appeared in the following print and online publications: "Memory, June 1942" in *Attic* in 2007; "Riding to the Anti-War March, New York City, March 20, 2004" on *Baltimore Indymedia* in 2006 and "Automation of Sleepwalkers" and "Caution for Monuments" on *Baltimore Indymedia* in 2008; "Vantage on a Saturday" (as "Reflections on a Saturday") in *Free Verse* in 2008; "Childhood From a Car" and "I Saw the Moon" in the *Goose River Anthology 2008* (Goose River Press: ME); "Sunspots," "To a Co-Worker (While Drinking a Beer)" and "Depression at 7 A.M." in the *Loch Raven Review* in 2006, 2007, and 2008 respectively; "I Saw the Moon" and "A World Without Picasso's Guernica" in *Le Nouveau Monde Vert* in 2008; "I Saw the Moon" in *Manorborn* in 2008; "Meditation on Washington D.C. in April 2003," "Poem for the Living," "Questions Rising Like Smoke" (as "Rereading Robert Bly's The Light Around the Body"), "Reading Adrienne Rich's Dark Fields of the Republic," "Sight," "S.U.V. With Landscape," "Urban Renewal," "War Mongers," "While You're Shopping, Bombs Are Dropping," and "A World Without Picasso's Guernica" all in *Poems Against War: A Journal of Poetry and Action* from 2003 through 2008; "S.U.V. With Landscape" in *Raving Dove* in 2008; and "That Movie Was So to Die For" in *This Poem Is Sponsored By: Poems in the Face of Corporate Power* (Corporate Watch: UK) in 2007.

I: LANDSCAPE

Minás, *Vacancy*, Mixed media on canvas, 2007

Do what you know, and perception is converted into character.

> Ralph Waldo Emerson
> from *The Method of Nature*

WORDS

Plunging harpooned whales,
haul us through internal lights,
snap utopias.

WAR MONGERS

Are they slaves to harbored pain
or its invested captains?
Which words sail before the bullets?

Today we scramble for the lottery ticket
in history's scrapyard
where all must work.

Tomorrow our hands hold up the bridge
that allows the army to rumble through
and we only mumble, why us?

Do they smirk when wielding words
or are they welded by words?
Which forged talents gird their locked ships?

Now a march, like a spring of cicadas,
parades with placards of peace,
singing: All is possible.

A WORLD WITHOUT PICASSO'S *Guernica*

February 5, 2003

At the United Nations, blue drapes sheath
a tapestry rendition of *Guernica*, so speakers can paint
blitzkrieging dreams, burying screams affixed and aired;
killing machines can work again without fear.

Who expunged *Guernica* from the U.N.,
and then did U.N. walls tremor
down to their foundation
in the "war to end all wars"
and covetous twentieth century?

Yesterday, today, or tomorrow
bombs drop and discombobulated body parts
hurl through the air, and brown limbs
burst from horses
and spin past a still-standing bystander
dumbstruck
as infernos smoke and buildings crumble.

WHILE YOU'RE SHOPPING, BOMBS ARE DROPPING

Saturday sun
details faces
of marchers and watchers.
We are shouting "no" to normalcy.

        While I'm speaking,
        bombs are nearing.

And meeting friends for dinner tonight
I'll still have my life to solve:
Whom do I love, and who loves me?

        While we're breathing,
        bombs are cleaving.

Solidarity with
fathers, sisters, neighbors, strangers
is how I live,
is what I can give.

SIGHT

Image seen through a photographer's still, mute frame:
An Iraqi Sunni grandmother, granddaughters flocked around her,
grins—her rooted teeth healthy and
glinting in the flinty light against
tan summer dust and her own purple headscarf;
local Shiite militia were rebuffed
from confiscating her family's house.

This tale of tribal tug-of-war shall not end well:
Tomorrow walking back from market
assassins' guns crater her robed body
in red clatter. None witnessed the incident,
notes an American soldier to the photographer.
Her Sunni heritage is not discernable
in an upper set of dentures
still on the dusty ground.

POEM FOR THE LIVING

I:
Vows slip from stacked newspapers
like subscription mailers no one wants: They swirl under cars,
wrap around posts, flutter down
                                    mucked with dirt and exhaust;
pile on sidewalks, a sea of stained papers. At dusk,
I scramble over garbage to get back home.

II:
        Orderly squads of soldiers
        pass crowds in business casual
        to invade overseas for oil.

        Under a Saturday March sun
        parading draws shoppers and children
        as dogs lope through nubile buds.

        Dark sedans of decision-makers
        blow red lights to reach meetings
        while reporters tail celebrities.

        Photojournalists frame icons
        for people sleeping in neon
        dreaming of sexy stardom.

        The workweek rehauls itself
        onto buses, subways, into cars,
        as elsewhere populations snapshot to dust.

III: March 20, 2003
When bombs dropped far away, rain came the next day
        to the U.S. Capital, a gray drain
seeming to say the whole world would pay.

In a small room I woke beside my lover,
        but my bones
hijacked my mouth and said, "Mass Murder."

We refused to work that day Iraq was attacked.
        We cooked, kept home.
Outside, justice crept into underground bulbs.

Birds on the street
        argued with song
as if they did not belong.

Human screams, attached to dust, began traversing the earth.

IV:
I vigil by the White House to answer with stillness,
 "No Civilian Bombing" stenciled on a sign, squared in my lap . . .
until lullabies of evening strollers eddy past
through the layered glow and breezy leaves
of this ceremonial place. Nearing the placard
passers' chittar-chatter
collapses like bridges
imploded to air
as life drifts off
beyond the blackness
like cool winds touching down here, hinting
of the cold singleness of stars
and weaving off
into the vast elsewhere. Night is more spacious
than all our hearts;
in this space hearts can listen.
Human-perfected bombs
fall on praying families
in my person.

Evening tunnels to a dark of plums.

                                            continued...

V:
Norma O'Malley waddles to the door;
two o'clock light sleeps on Iowa June wheat.
She's sixty-two, a rooted widow, and her son
Bill, whom she loves more than the sun,
plans to greet more than the dawn,
for whom she knits socks though he's forty-two—

Ms. O'Malley soon may shake
like a tree branch torn by an overfull river
and wedged taut across two rocks.
The news ricochets from field
command to base, and then from desk to desk.
It nears her door. . . . It shatters now.

VI: Diana
"Dear diary, this dorm room
is what I control: four square walls
with Sara-Beth, who comes and goes blithely,
sequined and sequenced. But I can't rush out
today, have skipped my classes—the whole reason I moved
here to New York City. I need to be
indoors, dressed in sweats, stripped
of architectural prettiness, how my mother raised me,
and write of what I've only heard. But how?
I'll meditate upon a star, a zone where anyone can hide.
Stars soon to come out, do they tinsel a bombed-out building
in Fallujah? Is it night there now
and do I rotate under the same light
to where a chair
blasted into the street
invites me to sit?

Did they live there, like me—
in some Apartment 4B—smally?"

VII: Cape Cod
Flags flap from houses.
Tuesday's concert includes a patriotic song.
The gray newspaper armors its tones.
August rolls on.

Ocean rumbles through slicing mist.
Faintest clouds touch green dunes.
Birds chime from slightly tossed pines.
This is my home.

Opinions are honed like thin knives.
Puddles of silence coalesce in gutters;
on clear days they catch the sun's multicolors.
Watch the changes.

VIII:
Blood, seep into the fruit tree
alone in the desert of neon, desert of sirocco wind,
desert of televisions, desert of farmers' almanacs,
fallow of public speaking, reservoir of private censure,
and circulate the harvest, share this strange fruit.

A few have joined us, pass around the circle.
Wind, whirl incense of this wild wholeness
over oceans, needle through blocked mountains,
rush silent deserts, infuse tents and houses,
and widen the circle, coax more to sit among us
to share the suffusion, sumptuous with nutrients:
this vision of the fruit tree, fruit tree's vision,
vision of the apple seed, the whole apple.

MEMORY, JUNE 1942

To describe a boat at dawn
with flowers, yellow flowers
raining down

is to describe my father
waiting for us to fish
before I went to war.

CHILDHOOD FROM A CAR

Finding my first home,
I slow as red-yellow leaves
swirl around the door.
Revving off, in the rear-view
a strong dog bounds into view.

PRACTICE

Looking for smooth stones
to arrange on my window
an order of loss.

BALMY

Who moved spade-shaped leaves,
these bruised greenings on the trees,
to sway so slowly?

SUNSPOTS

Cloud drift speckles leaves;
a plane writes across the sky . . .
I have traveled far.

A light-burst knifes me.
I plunge through memory chutes
back to this garden.

Behind me, windows
of my friend's house shine with sheer
unblinking brightness.

His blue swimming pool—
diving through humid, blank air
I'm fluid as grass.

OCTOBER RAIN

Toads squat, calm on palms,
as a gray pointillist's mist
enshrouds their chilled ponds.

Daylong, their cocked arms
spar the drizzle, like docked skiffs.
All clears soon enough.

URBAN RENEWAL

Broken gutter glass
snags sun, grows infused like grass,
glints with criss-crossed dreams.

LONG DISTANCE RUNNER

John runs each day past droopy rowhomes
and nudging grass in parks and yards
to mold his legs more strong and hard,
for this year has been a hurricane
as his mother died, then dad collapsed
from a sudden heart attack, but now
wheezes in bed at home. John pounds
the ground with their stupendous loss,
which arrived like wind, blowing down
his parents early, and left a sky
so clear and permanent and vast
that he engrafts this panorama
into his running, threading the past
through footsteps, owning it, as he
pushes through middle age to hear
some second-wind on his fortieth year.
He jogs a mile on cold cement.
October winds rehearse their toss
of white snow, as if banking windows,
but leave the city shinier, glossed,
and tearing down last colors as
the cars and buses lumber home
and spray the night with neon. John
just home from work himself, lets go
of work-thoughts grinding into his stride,
and thinks of Fran—four months now married—
who might be home by now to whip
up dinner in their house they bought
in a rebounding neighborhood
called Waverly, in Baltimore,
to get in while the getting's good,
as housing prices outpace incomes,
for who knows why, he thinks—*except
the world is getting crowded, scarce.*
      "Watch it, buddy," some jarhead barks,
and butts his shoulder into John's,
so John jerks back in ricochet
while running forward—now glancing behind.

continued...

   Nut job, John mutters, but doesn't utter,
a trick of living in the city
where speaking can make truth a fool.
A tide of cars exhales from work
as cabs are jostling, weaving through.
The pizza place he passes hums
with yellow warmth. He jumps across
a stack of today's newspapers, stops
outside the local bookstore, scans
through glass in a nostalgic flash
of days he read all afternoon.
Legs pump—and now upon his toes,
he turns and circles home, and as
he sprints, the day's events reshow
as hindsight on the route now passed.
Confusion orders to this dash.
He halts a block from home and walks,
then stretches, feels as if he sees
the way backward, and so ahead.
He bumbles in. "Hey Fran," he squawks,
still hyper with post-run adrenaline,
and Fran—still in her work clothes—peeks
from the kitchen door while simmering peas
and tofu, steaming up the room,
her turn in their divided chores.
    "How was it?"
        "Good," he says, and feels
so easeful watching her as dusk
twines through her hair . . . feels more at ease
than any time this year. Eyes lock.
Release. Fran notes that John seems present
more than usual, without the fog
of worry he's been pushing through
and past. She thinks: *I've never had
to doubt his stamina and drive
to thread his own way and arrive
at where we both can reconcile
amid this maze of teeming life*

a simple home from all the things
bestowed and forced on us by the world.
The wind slaps the hall window where
he stands. He showers upstairs, descends,
and she brings dinner out, two beers.
They eat, exchange some gentle nods,
unwrinkled smiles, then bantered hopes;
relish their talk, warm up, presaging
anointment in the evening where
they weave their miniature of the world.
They read a bit, and climb in bed.
He comes to her, and they make love,
like a low flame in a long winter,
or kite that nears a mountaintop.

AUGUST HIKE IN BALTIMORE

We thread beneath young oak and beech,
winding our way beyond car noise
into the shadowy, older woods
where thick, tall trees catch slabs of light,
and work, commuting, daily news
dissolve in the early Sunday cool
and light suspended in the air
immerses us in stillness. There
cocooned in a mesh of speckled leaves
we find a sidetrail log and sit
to share mid-morning sandwiches
of cheese, tomato, Italian bread,
and touching hands while sharing, we
embroider ourselves together like
the braided songs of scattered birds,
a free music for a free world.
Then off again, treading the trail,
we relax into its curves and bumps,
and breathing in the cleaner air,
acclimate to the given world.
We stop on a bridge. I soak up the sun;
you tuck in the shade, and we both watch
some dogs plashing about a creek
barking and swimming, having fun,
and people gazing from the shore
in slowness steeped in heat and light.
A butterfly meanders like
a drunken balloon above the sand,
which glints with yellows becoming whites,
while we linger, lapping up the scene
in the staircase of rising August heat.
The sun bores down upon the bridge
in a noon cone of widening light
that sucks us both into its breath,
arouses our cells, summons sweat.
We decide to go, our water low,
back to the car, and then back home.
Retracing, we find a fork in the trail

and choose the way you think is right,
while knowing both will get us there
in this urban park, which transported us . . .
though it is just an isle of wild
amid the world that's ordered outside—
more ordering, than order yet—
and not as whole as this green order.
By the reservoir's soft waterfall,
we reach the pavement, find the car,
and glancing back, I look to see
a tan tree-trunk, sculptural, dead,
still poised upon the dam's stone ledge
as water trickles past and down
into the shallow creek below
that mumbles beside the parking lot
into the city. We drive home.
I make a lunch, then you nod off,
and I head to a coffee shop
to read some deeply ingrained words,
and hearing another sound themselves
delve deeper into my own core,
igniting a reservoir of feeling
beneath the cooling summer dusk
and green leaves resting from the heat
in a pitter-patter of breezy mirth.
As feelings ooze, I feel as if
a breeze extends from my fingertips
in a two-way passage with the wind,
and through ebbing and flowing, we connect.
The sky evolves to cobalt blue
and my outdoor table sharpens, as if
the intertwining twinkling lights
signal an intermingled world.
Through finding others, grows my heart.
I must tend myself and those I love,
I note, and gathering to go,
return to the literature on hand
to sip and mull a last few words
attune to the butterflying world.

11: COMMUTING THROUGH DARKNESS

Minás, *Hide and Seek*, Mixed media on canvas, 2006

Every stave in a picket fence should be drawn with wit, with wit of one who sees each stave as new evidence about the fence. The staves should not repeat each other. A new fence is stiff, but it does not stand long before there is a movement through it, which is the trace of its life experience. The staves become notes, and as they differ the wonder of a common picket fence is revealed.

>						Robert Henri
>						from *The Art Spirit*

VANTAGE ON A SATURDAY

Shock-booms from internecine wars
echo in the alley like faces of prison guards
where I park my car, and at five-thirty before dawn
each weekday twist the key for work.

On the highway, a gluttony of strangers
in metal cages joust and cushion one another
journeying to the officialdom of garages and offices,
phone calls and lunch. An unseen sun
alofts, now sets. Music pressed to discs
sits in apartments, and triggered at dusk
wafts into the air, altering perceptions
of air and space, walls and windows.
Night luminesces. So there you are—
my dialogue with heroes long dead,
dreams like panthers at the zoo,
a wind of shadows rushing across earth.

This Saturday I can dance
if I want to. The bright sun illuminates the brick
and concrete of city facades like so many barred windows
I have helped construct.
Where does freedom go? Shall I seek it?

TO A CO-WORKER (WHILE DRINKING A BEER)

> *Be the change you want to see in the world.*
> Mahatma Gandhi

Driving to work, I'm trying to steer
toward rational disappointment with the world;
let's not conduct a discussion

now. Outside the office
sparrows dive-bomb for scraps;
their March songs are sustaining, exploding with cheer,

while behind the horizon, container ships
spider across the earth's oceanic breasts
to the tune of calculated hopes and fears.

And who am I? A soloist singing
from a divine score, as contend both shills and seers?
My aria starts at five to drive to work.

Tonight I hope she calls—or that I do.
I make frozen pizza, beans and salsa on the side.
I read Gandhi in a nostalgic dream.

So you have a new wife, baby boy almost here,
and a different tale—I wish you well—one Caruso
to another, waving clearly as the fog rolls in.

I SAW THE MOON

I saw the moon this morning
driving in darkness on the highway to work. I had forgotten
I lived on a planet. The moon swooned across my windshield
and swung—so to speak—into the passengerside window. I tried
to glimpse, peruse its pinkish marbled hue
and swerved twice into the left-hand lane,
coming too close to change.
I had to forget the moon.
Tend the machine
entrusted at hand.

The moon appeared again—mammoth,
primordial, aglow, father of o-shapes,
mother of a million bats kissing a fulfillment of wishes
few know they have. I find the moon again while moving
from Highway 95 onto the circular Washington Beltway, and feel
renewed by this coincidence, circling the moon, refreshed
in the waters of what I am, not through the memory of events,
but through the memory of roots.
Thirty miles traveled—the moon
now exudes a lemony-milky hue:
a succulent descent
into a wide open cradle
where wild things are born
in the glow of the night
some call a wakeful dream.

S.U.V. WITH LANDSCAPE

He polishes, buffs.
They were wrong. Spring spawns through hard
ground. *Who's on top now?*

Highways ribboning
the land are paved with crushed rose.
Monoshaped summery

malls beckon; birds mass
by windows. As he drives, droves
blink back through mirrors.

I'll pass all. The slow,
recurring workweek small-talks
to mounting Fridays—

Each dawn he revs his
private war, tanks past surnamed
cul-de-sacs, eats lunch

disgorged from packets,
programs data terminals.
At home, the news says:

>   Ripe bombers harrow the earth;
>   they sow the earth with pebbles of dream,
>   and open arms aria
>   to be lifted, and roses
>   are rising into the sky,
>   ushering past porous clouds
>   like tears from unshed tears.

MANEUVER FOR POSITION

after Bradley Walker Tomlin

```
I have a lesson.
                                              I have a question.
                        Answer.
                        Accept it.
Are you welcome?
                                              Will you listen?
                        Never relent.
Always repent.
                                              Expand the event.

                        Responsibility.
                        Come with me.

Sad or happy?
                                              Mystery.
                        History!
        Debate.
                                              Create.
                    Relate.
                                              Mistake.
                        Peekaboo,
I like you.                                   Boohoo.

                        Stand.

Where?                                        There.
                        Aware.
(Not here.)                                   (Yes near.)
                        Need.
Then!                                         Again.
                        Win.
Friend.                                       Feed.
                        Begin.
```

TITLE YOURSELF

I have other pursuits and you are nosy.
This poem bores you—snores in your ear.
I won't employ a single word well.

I know where you stand. I listen to your footsteps
across these tercets. I lounge and laugh off-stage.
I dream in the hot, black mouth of a volcano,

and if you squibble your eyebrows (I can see),
I'll curtain behind this clause, and at most sense
your offish eyes like some sharp afternoon

light blaring against drawn curtains, illuminating
dust on chairs. How I dance in my apartment!
But look, time's tight. I have to catch my train

to work (in trade publishing now). If only
I could escape this dreary line.
(There is so little time for conversation).

DEPRESSION AT 7 A.M.

      Minimal—like a banner—
greets commuters at subway stations, waves
over the capital, is bunting behind the candidate
as she speaks, appears as a T-shirt logo
on some dude sipping a soft drink.
Fists squeeze satisfaction out of lattes, from whizzing past
cars on the expressway, by getting in line
first.

      Churning the world, skimming
off the top, siphoning crème de la crème
into gated communities, commerce processes us,
though the gears grind slower, like a children's Ferris wheel
everyone clings to, yet most are beyond
three feet tall. We should be doing
something better, more adult, but gawk
here, while the wheel slows—in fact it stopped long ago—
and feet dangle,
millions of idle feet
      letting their shoes drop.

      Old song—
how did you come to this?
Today the refrain is "too late,
off to work now, I can't wait
until dinner."

SONG FOR THE EARTH

I.
The experiment in mind control

                          is working!

Automated landscapes prove

                          we do not revolve around the sun!

Earth is disappearing—methodically replaced by

                          EVERYWHERE.

Tunes crooned in basement laundry rooms:

                          a new spiritual. . . .

Where to run
           when abandoned railroad stations become

                          the new dance craze?

How to think when

           plastic surgery patients talk about the bible

                      of their new spic-and-span lifestyle?

        All the running tracks have been purchased!

They are branded

           with grandfather clock names

                        wound continuously circular.

The obvious is so hard to get a hold of. . . .

        Where is the door handle?

                Could it be among Allen Ginsberg's

half destroyed

        stunned and amazed pages?   Or Emerson's opus

mulled on a brisk autumn walk

        surveying bespeckled woods . . .

                how we all got here,

how Walt Whitman

        rose out of Brooklyn

                like Poseidon

with a heart of steel and sunflowers

        offering nurses' tears

                and a banjo's jubilee

to any willing reader for

        journey through time's flower

                to peel appearance

                      continued...

    from reality

                and skin ourselves

                              to eat this return

again to where we are now

                    riding a river

        upon rafts of memory and forgetfulness.

II.

        In my work-week
        I often speak

        to just five or six
        assorted persons,

        such passing bits
        it can be knit

        together solely
        through some vision.

        Out there, the vastness
        through which I pass

        mostly is glimpsed
        from reading the paper.

        Who can capture
        on a blank page—

        not abstractions—
        but an idea of things?

III.
Let me travel now, slowed down
to the edge of a blackened crater, and peer past
charred cliffs into the rumbling slumbering volcano—
anonymous black gunk, indistinct genesis among us—
and here anchor my imagination.

IV.
An old bus rattles
through city streets
stuffed with tired riders
as night blankets homes
and a few crickets intone
to each person let go.

The first spring Saturday
of farmer's market
welcomes city dwellers,
and the wily and wakeful
trot out their joy
before the harvest again.

MEDITATION ON WASHINGTON D.C. IN APRIL 2003

During the war, winter thawed in a rapid
of hot and cold days, disarming us
with a tempest of wind, lull, and rain:
Walking to work in a wetness of caves,
talking of war in flash fountains of sun,
greens filled the trees like so many birds;
birds will perch soon like so many buds;
they will sing the ever-fresh song.

So this land filled with its own sunrise—
petaled origami of purple, a dogwood painter's-brush
of white—and people entered the landscape
as days grew longer, spring misted toward
summer, and sun suckled life; yet in Iraq
where battles were "victorious," already blazed
summer, crisping cities and deserts a-swirl
with rumor, wind, dust-ups and explosions.

All April thin winds slipped around dogwoods
and spread ribbons of coolness upon the blooming
reminding that winter still kernelled in wind and soil;
newspapers in metal boxes tolled destruction;
people on their free day pursued their peace
or pleasure, goals or strife, and May's reborn.

I crouch down to a white chrysanthemum and note
how underground rivers purl the whole globe,
where history's hands too are weavers in the roots
and only spring's return reveals each cycle's results.
A fuzzy, cream sweetness tickles my nose.
Flowers leap into wide, drinking eyes.

Shall the Iraq war retreat to history books, like a nightmare
enters language to be soothed when told? Or does time
teach a lesson other than hope?
How do we recognize when a new history
begins, like an infant mewling a preface
to dialogue, or juggernaut's urge?

CAUTION FOR MONUMENTS

Before you seize some echoing ground
where flowers, hummingbirds and families gather
and entomb it in a monument, ponder
the monumental message.

How clearly sighted was the past
before the past was painted and captioned
by officious conductors
to control the future.

AUTOMATION OF SLEEPWALKERS

Skyscrapers aspire to earn their names
electrifying a twentieth century of perpetual dawn.

Rooms and pockets amass with mesmerizing screens
and soon fewer detect scents and wed hands.

People seek refuge in the mechanics of language,
foresaking significance; it does not require knives
to cut them to size.

The now of the street accelerates
as if cities are teeth of invisible cogs, conveying
all through an unspoken gate,
or did I mean fate,
or is this din appetite?

AGE WITHOUT HEROES

Known heroes loomed in bronze memorials,
grinned in scholarly books on alphabetized shelves,
while we met every dare with smirks and chuckles,
lingered at the cinema and sipped apéritifs.

Big blimps advertised ten-step salves
for aspirational aches.
We groomed second faces
and peacocked like kings.

Yet in the spotlight of the sun so common
few noted, untold heroes gave off sparks
which gasped toward fire. If light ever causes masks
to crack, some will name this pain healing, others hate.

THAT MOVIE WAS SO TO DIE FOR

Suck the lights down:
landscape of immaculate Barbie Dolls
tarred and feathered and taught to sing,
and gymed men chesting with lobotomized anger,
all dancing around a plot's pinwheel, pastiche'd
from art genres and processed through focus groups
to generate pornography.

Desire extracted from hope and secured in test tubes,
mixed to combust as images on a screen,
concludes with four people dead and one young woman
staring into the distance in a five-thousand-dollar pantsuit.

In a dawn erased of all you know
roll the credits of all you are not.
Inhaled like a mushroom cloud, cinema
dissipates, and you exit the projected stage
to a dinner of tining forks and laughter buried
by a procession of beer
arriving from the bar
translucent as holy candles
refracted in thick glass. Exterminate yourself.

NEW HUCKSTERS

Through medusa media, tongue-tied scientists
candy-coat eyes to hawk anorexic dreams,
and soon you have purchased a ticking debt
for the tomb of your possessions, or maybe
you just sweat at the laundry-mat of desires.
Fire in every mortgaged house and bedroom
has been funneled to release
smoke at nightclubs, and laughter
above the all-night burning echoes
through the drawn knives of ghettos.
The world in your hand, like a fledging
from a children's book, flutters,
and its stupefied and confused eyes
look up at you and wonder, what will you do?

MISTER X MUSES IN THE MIRROR

The blue above the hotel
is silent as my acts.
I watch a few clouds brew,
awaiting furtive facts.

Tonight I'll sample bars,
and rib local residents.
I like to sip the views
of armchair presidents.

Tomorrow, Europe-bound,
on a consulate nametag,
I'll mule memorandum
in a diplomatic bag.

There wined and dined, I'll lounge.
A target sleeps for me.
Such bureaucratic planning—
bottling normalcy.

Truly my friends, I'm bored,
languishing here alone,
encased by the drooled words
of paycheck-powered drones.

This whole façade clanks on,
and I'm a gagged linchpin.
Sometimes I just want waves
of murder to begin.

I lust to see mayhem
shatter public places,
the teeth of oiled machines
unleashing all our faces.

III: LIGHT

Minás, *Peacewriter*, Pencil on paper, 2003

Let a man have a profession for which God formed him that he may be useful to mankind to the whole extent of his powers, that he may find delight in the exercise of his powers, and do what he does with the full consent of his own mind.

Ralph Waldo Emerson
from *Sermon 143*

MUSIC OF QUESTIONS

Docked at a cafe table after voting on Election Day, hearing
the coarse whir of the espresso machine, slipstream of voices,
and dreamy electronic music intermingling in this *Common
Grounds* coffee shop, packed but cozy as a quilt, so everyone
intermeshes while pursuing their own path—I'm reading,
interweavng through reading, probing
questions supposedly solved,
asking: What is justice?
Am I threading the right path?
Do I recognize my footsteps?
Soon I will be submerged again in daily affairs,
but this here is music, the music of questions,
questions orbiting, widening my purview, focusing
the scope of what must be chosen and lived.

READING ADRIENNE RICH'S *Dark Fields of the Republic*

Warm indistinct midwinter, reading
Dark Fields of the Republic in wide white light
of a double-windowed coffee shop, luxurious in languor,
with rock-and-roll coming from the staff-run stereo, composing
notes *about the situation*, notating
in worn corduroys all afternoon, as others rush
in and out, eyes shaded below hats. Where will my path
excavate to? At the adjoining table, a bearded bulky dude
in blue jeans and jean-jacket talks about his paintings . . .
symmetry of birds,
grasped straws of soaring.
Outside, Friday's empty late afternoon
casts the sidewalks in painted quiet, not visibly registering
change of consciousness in ink. I am sending love.
Broadcast this:
who was in charge of definitions
and who stood by receiving them?
Enter the root
Throw all else away.
Cores are for unearthing, journey, and play.
Here is the street. You are the turn-off.
The light seems familiar, blank,
and astounding. Today
if you took the turn-off
it was for you.

SELF PORTRAIT AT THIRTY ONE

I.
Beyond the mind's cage, zone
without words: Mudflats of yellow bubble and burst
with brown and orange dust. This is why I gaze at art
in Washington D.C. at the National Gallery, to flash another's light
into the darkness of myself. A father
who dresses as if at a job called *Saturday*
says to his son, "I could have done that." People queue through
museum halls wearing belts of salaried jobs. I see camouflaged
soldiers pouring out of baseball caps. I see
the whole "murderous twentieth century" culminating
in discount family dinners at Caesar's Steakhouse.
It is American "reality" television, guest-starring
everyone, called *Survivor: Land of the Philistines*.
Yet I was looking at yellow, clay yellow, scooped raw
out of the earth, drenched by rain, then distilled
into pigment, and now congealed, like my life,
here and now. Or is this yellow my emotional sky—
or the painter Clyfford Still's yellow certainty?—
and there are explosions. Explosions of what?

II.
If you slap words on it,
splatter words all over it like black paint,
you won't be able to see because of the brightness.
Words can be bright—this simile fudged,
though yes they do splatter. If you scour
the canvas, denude it of color, emerges a force field
like a wall of sound, with fissures that throb
wider and narrower, as vertical bars
pulsate up and down. These bars, like lungs,
thicken and thin. No dictionary here—just a red sun,
though not a sun as the metaphor embeds—yet certainly red;
plus one stroke of yellow-white lightning, fossilized, a scar.
It all forms a contrast, which exhales . . .
and the bridge to here has many directions,
though the bridge pretends to span solely one way,
while all the other ways are very interesting. So beware,
beware of the bridge. Like the lock on your door,
you may cling to it for life.

continued...

III.
I have limped here, an older man
than I'll be soon at thirty-two, camping out
on a floodplain, where crossing rivers
have flooded and drained to reveal
the rich detritus of plans
in the muck of work and circumstance.
Flotsam and jetsam—from this
to parse, shape, and make stand
a two-bedroom house that represents the mind,
an acropolis for the modern human
who having lost . . . never has lost. Paintings
at the Hirshhorn Museum speak to me
on one of my trips to Washington D.C.
as a ragged, sometimes giddy refugee
from all I thought might, or would be,
who must build a temple of the familiar
to recognize myself in this factotum,
and within this safe interior space
descend down chthonic roots
to proffer gratitude
to vibrations at the core of the world.
> In the sculpture garden, bronze faces
> and abstract metals pose beneath spring's first pink;
> balconies of bird song
> terrace this sunken, rectangular atrium;
> blueness above is sailed by thin, delicate clouds
> as a gust touches my leg, a sculpture, then rustles off.

Will I take this moment with me into the next life,
that is the life commencing when I arise
from this park bench and leave here?

IV.
At the intersection
of two Latino teen girls in hot pink pants
and an older couple—Bosnian refugees—coughing out
    a conversation,
and four lanky kids horsing around and pushing each other
    in an imaginary corn field
is a square room with four directions leading toward five paintings
by Clyfford Still: *January 1951, 1960, 1948-C, 1962-D, 1960-R* —
opaque appellations
labeling portals
to a force-field, which extends
conjoining, colliding, overlapping, pulsing by
through walls and lives,
yet one cannot remain aloof
observer for too long. So humanity
inhabits two worlds
like a Hindu statue with six arms
waving with motions that whisper *enter*,
make me one. In paintings are shapes:
depictions of sound. Skeletons
of sound: partitioned impressions
of wavelengths. Pulsing wavelengths strobe
toward us like an atomic waterfall, pouring
through the body like red water, and it all seems
a perpetual red field; the original droplet
may rise back again. It is like death,
this life now opened.

continued...

V.
Is the whole point to heal?
Or did we begin this journey just to arrive home?
Is it the first home we are rebuilding, trying to resurrect
what was torn by the big bang
of birth into being? Are we bees
always mending honeycomb onto honeycomb,
growing a hive
that might in architecture sing
like the music we never heard
during our invisible eons
just before we departed
for the entangled dance,
arriving tainted and stained
with what we left
as we morphed into
the web of the womb.

RIDING TO THE ANTI-WAR MARCH, NEW YORK CITY, MARCH 20, 2004

From beneath earth's eastern curve, two rays—
one flat pink and one a higher, wider band of yellow—
cross the blue-awakening sky. They soar through reconstituting blue
as people mill outside a dusty, Baltimore meeting hall
waiting for two buses to carry us all
from under this cold canvas of light.

In the highway ducts
of New Jersey, below a blue
large as a celestial fingertip, we drive past
webs of steamy electrical works, a stream's trickle
through mustard-yellow grass, pass
a metal bridge, dip through marsh
fermenting beneath a vast grid of pipes,
all under a sky unique and tranquil
like any other day—
the world must change.

This road again, and my life
scaffolded in order to craft
another rung of a ladder
I construct so I can climb.
Ahead: Manhattan's ascendant skyline.
Alongside: Yellow-blue smog hovers over
octopi-shaped electrical generators; and here comes
a hill of houses, a steeple, what looks like mounds of garbage,
before we edge through a tollbooth, and the sun-brightened chill
ripens toward noon.

continued...

Deja vu against a window—
for a year ago I came here to march
against a nascent war, now launched.
So the world's river bucked, and now
the sun pinches like a decision
that will make the earth shudder
before being absorbed and merged
as birds gather on a dusty riverbed
none have seen run for a thousand years.

As the bus descends into the Lincoln Tunnel,
white clouds meld themselves into patches of blue:
twisting above, ribboning to white threads, mixing with blue,
dissipating beneath the sunblast.
We slip below, disappearing
into the tunnel's open mouth, and then we
rise in Manhattan
to chant our voices to be heard.

In a rented room
a couple builds
toward permanence.

On the street our dawn
goodbyes rise over cars
not to be divided.

In London,
two people scale Big Ben and hoist a banner:
"Time for Truth."

I blow on a cup of coffee,
last Saturday morning. *I'm searching inside,
constructing a way.*

When we hold hands, will we
become a photograph, or
new nexus?

At the march: A blur of silk and brass
Korean peace dancers spiral
around gongs and drums, as pink and black
radical cheerleaders
rewrite chants for a sailed-for dawn, while gray
paperheads from *Guernica*
nailed to sticks
sail above the crowd to the tune
of an eight-piece Dixieland brass-band, which incites
boogie-woogie. The band
drops back, docks
on the sidewalk, circling
a flock of listeners and dancers; a coronet's crescendo
fades behind
the crowd's tide
flashing forward. The day
folds into a core
small as a far-off star
and explodes
in a brief light-trail:
a comet's tail
speckled with each of us.

PORTRAIT OF HOME

My dearest painting in the other room, a piano's groovy tincture
ripples from the stereo. The apartment becalmed as we both work,
city blurred in repetitive rain—I have more than I can name and
as rhythmic breathing vessels we flow
through what must be arranged
into what we own.

UNKNOWN SOLDIER

for David Eberhardt

In green flak jacket with peace signs
pinned to both sleeves, a poet performs and says "I am
the unknown soldier, pouring blood." He himself poured blood
on draft cards forty-one years ago, then was pinned
into Lewisburg Federal Penitentiary for two-and-a-half years.
His hands tremble, pinch themselves until he pins
them behind his back—hand gripped in hand—
and notes how white phosphorous "made
by Dow Chemical" stuck to flesh to
burn "those Vietnamese," even underwater. Ingenuity
of our best and the brightest. How it sticks to him. How
paper and pen can tower over men. Tomorrow he will return
to his job helping destitute detainees meet bail. His journey's circle
cleanses him—but today, as history's waves leer and crash
with a low rumbled echo of menace and detritus, washing him
so clear-sighted he shakes, he speaks his poetry
before sixteen people on a Sunday, and the words quiver
like a finger sliding along a razor, back-and-forth
from rage to care . . . care to rage . . . rage to care.

SKETCH FROM A HILLTOP

Among the innumerable, scanning
from a hilltop far from dwellings, and on all sides a sea-floor
of tree-covered hills, except for a cut swath
cradling telephone lines, snaking up and down
and visible like the inside of a wave;
on a hill of dry, indistinguishable bushes and scattered pines
that opens to checkerboards of greening and dirt-brown clearcuts;
on a late morning perforated with silence
which freezes you if you can be touched and scattered—
for such days approach every life
like bird droppings pierce the forest floor,
dissolving down, feeding
shoots, which are eaten
by nibbling mice
that nourish wolves—
only who sought and went
know.

AGAINST *Guantanamo*

Know this: There is a jail offshore beyond
the law where U.S.-held suspects are tortured, where bound
without legal judgment, these men are caged for years,
experimented on through science's tears.
Dear Jorie Graham, your "moon" and opaque prose
in the crafted cage of your protest poem's pose
neither aids an Afghan peasant mistakenly held,
nor just tells a reader what this jail entails.

Proclaim this: A crime uncaging history's rue
was sanctified by barbarous wire and guns
as milling crowds mumbled in clouds of engorged fear
and comfortable cogs paced and wrung their hands
on tenement roofs (now condos). But we, yes
us here (for who else?) must build a better world.

FRAGMENT

And once the rains had flooded earth, and stopped,
receding like a sun-blocking, staircasing black flock
oblique into the sky, obdurate waters
withdrew. Islands of ground surfaced until
the sun repainted puddles. Land was wide
and echoless, unrolled to long horizons,
and marshy, with ovoid holes, where buildings once stood.
I stood, exhausted after two days work
unbarricading my cellar's hatch upon
noting new moss, which must have sensed the light.
Wading through garbage I found your crumbled house,
heard you below, and wedged off your basement door.
We stood in a silence of survivors, not one
person in view. Not one bird flew. And I,
who'd been on jury trial for efforts to halt
the government's slow march toward endless war,
began to smile. We held hands. With dawn's touch,
a rotunda of light encircled these umber plains;
and in four days, a mammoth migration thundered
behind the sunset. On the fifth night, while
gathering sticks and trash for campfire, under
an orotund rumble quaking the air, black wings
fragmented
                planetary lakes of red.

QUESTIONS RISING LIKE SMOKE

I.
... cowering behind
a boulder in a bird-loud valley
crouched above a tricking stream, caught
within the mind's-eye of a Hegelian historian—a troglodyte
heaves a stone, grunting syllables, at his double ...

Cities spiral from the ashes of campfires
and small armies spark and fade, while Plato's *Dialogues*
are smuggled into naves and caves.
At the crossroad, bread is traded
for thimblefuls of tea,
while on glimmering seas, ships weave
the world into a web,
and soon half-free people
encircled by whirling doves
elect leaders of fire and ice.

The world's din pierces clouds
until twentieth century world wars
smash half of civilization to dust.
A fog of silence englobes the ruins,
and questions rise like smoke before
dispersed by the dawning of televisions.

Skulls are squeezed
into statistics, and on spinning printing presses, reasons
are alphabetized across periodicals
to be recycled
into tomorrow's horror.

At a panel discussion on the poet Robert Bly, students lean
keenly in assigned seats to hear one professor drawl: "*The Light
Around the Body* is simply not
succinct, nor is the language
original. I.e., it's been said
before, and the line
breaks,
predictable."

continued...

II.
In a rent-stabilized apartment with clouds visible
through smudged windows, a grandmother
glimpses a falcon gliding
across the brown silhouette of New Jersey apartment towers,
now veering over the turgid Hudson, and circling
toward her mammoth Bronx shore.
On television, newscasters intone
in clipped sentences
fast as automatic weapons
and as dispassionate as automatic weapons
the fate of a world
circling toward war.

Beneath a tree on Gibson Island, Maryland, a boy hides
from his sister, playing tag. "You're it,"
she says. He falls dead.
His arms reach out
toward the sunset. Eyes closed, he lies
hush as the sky, then jumps up, resurrected
like tomorrow's sunrise
over a young soldier, who dreams
back home to Lincoln,
Nebraska, now bunked
in Charleston, South Carolina. This morning
these boys lazily rise, and the soldier tidies up,
chows down, and sighs
as he leaves on a sluggish gray battleship
toward the arid unknown
in the boredom of a weekday afternoon
when most are at school or work.

III.
The war debate abates
to who has the best smile,
while myriad printed opinions
befuddle neighbors' eyes,
until the avalanche
buries whispered *whys*,
frozen now as frowns
on faces all around.
Technologies survive
in the smolderings of hope
as trucks of fear arrive
with the new world order.

>   Who says a prayer?
>   Who kneels? What words can be said?
>   Who recalls prayers, regurgitates, spits
>   them on stone? Who watches what grow?

continued...

IV.
Newspapers rise in the air over Manhattan
as we debark from the bus, strangers
flooding the streets, shoulder
to shoulder in the March air
to meet now and march here
as the news flies away like falcons,
and shoppers slow down to watch
our slowness make room for the clarion call,
the call to stop wrestling with shadows
and begin the journey inward
to lead us to this street.

The truth snores in garbage cans
as pigeons peck around it, with gray coos,
before scattered by the stampede
of cacophonous blurred shadows
from which faces emerge
among 9th Avenue stalls,
faces that do not remind us of ourselves.

Have you stopped wrestling with angels?
Relinquishing—people grab their brother's leg
to twist it, and twist it
beyond when the brother says, "Uncle!"
twisting it with extra elbow juice
to make the mortar for their house.

In midnight alleys of mobbed solitude,
original fire streaks between people's eyes
as a tenant greets a potential landlord
assessing character as well as contract,
as lovers small-talk over dinner,
as a stranger pets a tied-up dog,
and a women punches a keypad,
yet pauses to greet smile with smile
in a drugstore checkout line.

We call the falcons back
and they flock down, beating light into pressed steel,
blowing back clouds, circling and screeching
into the silence; they drag an embedded nail
through the concrete of our conscience
as they circle slowly downward
into the commercial core of Manhattan, shrinking
their circumference, spiraling
between skyscrapers
to perch in fierce calm
on our gauntleted hand
where none apologize.

This is the mirror we must turn to fire,
burning down to essence,
living there, in the school among the ruins,
to pass through the procession of private dances,
relearning the economy of the gift.

END NOTES

✗ "While You're Shopping, Bombs Are Dropping" takes its title from a refrain chanted among a group of anti-war marchers, including myself, on Saturday, March 23, 2003, as we marched through New York City. We marched with tens of thousands of others protesting the 2003 U.S. invasion of Iraq.

✗ "A World Without Picasso's *Guernica*" recounts a true story of a tapestry rendition of Pablo Picasso's *Guernica* that hung outside the United Nations Security Council for years before the 2003 U.S.-led invasion of Iraq. Pablo Picasso painted *Guernica* in response to the German Nazi bombing of the Spanish town Guernica in April 1937. The Nazis bombed Guernica to help the Spanish Fascists prevail against leftist forces during the Spanish Civil War. The painting now hangs in the Prado Museum in Spain. In 1976, a tapestry rendition of the painting was placed outside the United Nations Security Council, donated by Nelsen Rockefeller, and it was shown there until 2003. On Feb. 5, 2003, a blue curtain covered this *Guernica* tapestry during then-U.S. Secretary of State Colin Powell's pivotal United Nations speech, which outlined a case for invading Iraq. Reporters and camera crews waiting to question Powell and other diplomats outside the U.N. Security Council photographed them against a blank blue backdrop, rather than against images of *Guernica*.

✗ "Maneuver for Position" is based on a painting of the same title by Bradley Walker Tomlin in the collection of the National Gallery of Art in Washington D.C.

✗ "Sight" is based on the true story of Iraqi woman Suaada Saadoun—as reported by Ashley and Joanna Gilbertson in "Last Photographs," *Virginia Quarterly Review* (Summer 2007, pp. 27-49).

✗ "Unknown Soldier" is for David Eberhardt. As a college student in 1967, Mr. Eberhardt poured blood on draft cards in Baltimore, Maryland to protest and stigmatize the draft for the U.S.-Vietnam war. He served over two years in prison for this act. Today he is active in his local progressive community and author of the poetry collection, *blue running lights* (Abecedarian Books, 2007).

ALSO BY GREGG MOSSON

Poetry
Season of Flowers and Dust

Anthologies and Journals (Edited)
Poems Against War: Music & Heroes (Wasteland Press, 2007)
Poems Against War: Ars Poetica (Wasteland Press, 2008)
Poems Against War: Bending Toward Justice (Wasteland Press, 2010)

ABOUT THE AUTHOR

Gregg Mosson is the author of *Season of Flowers and Dust,* a book of nature poetry from Goose River Press. He has published several issues of *Poems Against War*, a journal with national contributors.

His journalism, poetry, and literary criticism have appeared in *The Cincinnati Review, The Baltimore Review, The Baltimore Sun, The Oregonian, Loch Raven Review*, and *The Futurist*. His poetry was nominated for the Pushcart Prize in 2007 and 2009.

Gregg Mosson has an MA from the Johns Hopkins Writing Seminars, where he was a teaching fellow and lecturer. He has a BA in English from Portland State University. He was born in New York City.

You can visit him online at www.greggmosson.com.

Minás. *Masks*, Prisma color on paper, 1995

ABOUT THE ARTIST

Minás Konsolas forges everyday experience into contemporary archetypes by blending modern living and dreaming with mythology inspired by his native Greece. Reprinted here in mostly black and white are three colorful oil paintings, one black-and-white drawing, and one colored drawing: "Diminishing Returns" (cover), "Vacancy" (p. 9), "Hide and Seek" (p. 35), and "Peacewriter" (p. 57) and "Masks" (p. 84).

Konsolas develops his canvases by adding and eliminating multiple layers of paint. He creates his images by scraping and smearing, and this process allows him to paint and draw at the same time. He owns Minás Gallery, an art gallery and event space in Baltimore, Maryland, where many artists and writers enjoy a convivial forum. His gallery and art are online at www.minasgalleryandboutique.com.

www.ingramcontent.com/pod-product-compliance
Lightning Source LLC
Chambersburg PA
CBHW071838290426
44109CB00017B/1859